CHRISTMAS

WITH

Amanda Brunker

and

The Blue Haven Food Company

The
Blue
Haven
Food
Company

KINSALE

Published by

The Blue Haven Food Company

Pearse Street, Kinsale, Co Cork, Ireland

www.bluehavenfoodco.com

Photography: Marc O'Sullivan

Food stylist: Marie Phelan

Graphic design: Kieran O'Connor

© 2010 The Blue Haven Food Company

A catalogue record of this book is available from the British Library.

ISBN 978-0-9566738-0-0

Contents

Recipes:

Soups & Starters

Meat & Fish

Vegetarian Alternatives

Introduction

Happy Christmas, everyone and welcome to my first-ever cookbook!

I am so excited about this book as it combines three of my favourite passions: food, Christmas and, of course, entertaining!

As a traditionalist, I love the idea of spending time with family and friends at this time of year, so when it came to compiling this book, I knew I wanted to surround myself with a great team and good friends. And The Blue Haven Food Company were the obvious partners for me.

I first became friendly with the culinary team at The Blue Haven Hotel three years ago, after launching their Hamlets Café Bar in Kinsale. We immediately clicked, as we shared the same ethos about food and life: good food = good times! So I have been working quietly on the idea of a cookbook with them ever since.

Being a number one bestselling author myself (and a hungry one at that!), I wasn't prepared to serve up anything less than five-star recipes that are easy to prepare, fun to make and guaranteed to make you everyone's favourite person.

And while we all know that the festive season sometimes (sorry, always) can prove a little stressful, myself and the gorgeous guys, Jon Kenny and James Makin, from The Blue Haven Food Company have done our best here to give you the ultimate guide to Christmas entertaining.

Together, we cover all catering eventualities, from the girlie nights in, baking with the kids, St Stephen's Day suppers and New Year's Eve banquets, while not forgetting the main event itself in all its over-indulgent glory! Whether you're all about the turkey-feast or looking for something just a little bit different, I reckon we've got it covered.

Last, I just want to wish you well and thank you for letting me share this Christmas with you. I'm honoured that you chose us to make your party perfect and I look forward to hearing all your great success stories once I hit the road again.

Lots of love and Champagne Kisses

Amanda x

The Blue Haven Food Company

The Blue Haven Food Company is a dedicated catering and food manufacturing company based in Kinsale, the Gourmet Capital of Ireland. We specialise in Gourmet Food Products for the Retail and Hospitality Sector. We strive to make fabulous fresh food with flair, passion and excellence. Delicious, award winning and simply the best of Ireland's natural goodness.

Our signature products include our award winning "Fresh From Kinsale" Seafood Chowder and Fish Pie, as well as our collection of tasty patés including Smoked Salmon, Smoked Mackerel and Chicken Liver. We also produce a selection of Jams, Marmalades and an award-winning Honey and Mustard Dressing.

In the company's short existence we have won numerous awards, which we are very proud of. Our biggest accolade came in the form of winning 2 Gold Stars in the "Great Taste Awards" 2010 in the UK for our Seafood Chowder, which is an amazing accolade for a company that was only formed quite recently. This award reinforces our ethos of producing the best possible products using local and natural ingredients.

In Ireland, we have also won the "SHOP" 2009 awards for our Seafood Chowder. The "SHOP" judges deemed the product to be the best new Irish Food Product on the market, again we were overjoyed to see all our hard work being rewarded in such a way. A number of our other products were also recognised at the awards.

While these awards are very important to us, our main goal is always to offer you, the consumer, the best quality products available on the supermarket shelf, so please look out for our products in Supervalu and Centra, Dunnes Stores and many local independent retailers. You can also find our products in a number of Farmers' Markets in and around Cork.

If you would like to learn more about the Blue Haven Food Company, please see our website

www.bluehavenfoodco.com

The food company now operates a very successful catering business, so if you are having any type of event we would be more than happy to cater for all your culinary requirements!

The Blue Haven Hotel

The Blue Haven Hotel is a boutique-style hotel situated in the heart of Kinsale, Co Cork. This picturesque town is seasoned with Norman, Spanish and English influences, add one major battle and let simmer for 400 years. The result ... Ireland's fine food capital. But, the medieval town of Kinsale is not just about food, it's about traditional bars, beautiful buildings, narrow streets, colourful shops and galleries and lots of activities on sea and land. Kinsale is not just a place, it's a state of mind.

One of Ireland's best known hotels, the Blue Haven graciously combines Kinsale's charm of yesterday with the comforts of today. Our reputation for excellent food, friendly personal service and meticulous attention to detail will always ensure your visit to Kinsale's Blue Haven Hotel is a special one.

The Blue Haven Hotel has an array of dining options to choose from – from our cosy Blue Haven Café, to our luxurious Bar, Bistro and Restaurant. All dishes combine seasonal produce from our garden and fresh seafood from our local shores, carefully prepared by our team of international chefs. The hotel prides itself on delivering the ultimate in friendly and efficient service to our customers.

Over the years, the Blue Haven Hotel has developed into a collection that includes a tapas and wine bar, high quality restaurant, gastro bar, a number of cafés, a beautiful Georgian guesthouse, as well as the main hotel itself. Whatever your taste and requirements are, the Blue Haven Collection has the premises to meet and exceed your expectations.

Most recently, the Blue Haven Food Company has been developed and, as a result, we now bring you this fun and exciting Christmas cookbook. Our passion and love for fresh, tasty and high quality food can be seen throughout the book and we hope that you enjoy every recipe. Most importantly, we hope you have fun with the book and it makes your Christmas more memorable.

Merry Christmas from all at the Blue Haven Collection!

Cormac Fitzgerald   *Ciaran Fitzgerald*

PS: If you would like more information on the Blue Haven Collection, please see

www.bluehavenkinsale.com

Congratulations!

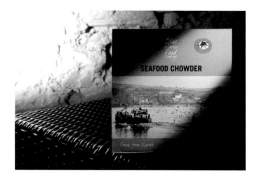

Enterprise Ireland is the agency charged with accelerating the development of world-class Irish companies so that they can compete and grow in world markets. As part of this we take an active interest in new food producers who have the vision to go the export development route. Innovative, heritage driven, high quality propositions, and above all great tasting food, backed up with high standards of food safety and hygienic production, are the prerequisites for Irish food producers to succeed abroad.

It is particularly gratifying to see the success of the Blue Haven Food Company which only emerged into the Irish retail scene in the past two years, rapidly gaining a reputation for great food, with strong branding and great taste. The recent success in the high-profile UK Great Taste Awards with the notable achievement of two gold stars at the first attempt is a strong endorsement of the company, the food and their future.

I wish the Blue Haven Food Company every success.

Garrett Dee

Senior Development Adviser

Consumer Foods

Fresh from the sea... fish the way it should be

13

Where to buy your ingredients

The rule of thumb on where to buy your produce is to get to know your main supplier, whether it's your local greengrocer, butcher or fishmonger. Do not be afraid to ask questions and to build up a relationship. You will find all producers are proud to tell you about the origin and benefits of their products. Be sure to ask about the best cooking methods and cooking times.

Furthermore, a good relationship can save you time and money, as a good local supplier will be happy to help where they can, whether it's trussing a bird for roasting or filleting a piece of fish. It is important to remember that each individual producer is an expert in their own particular field, so try to gain as much information as possible from them.

Over the last number of years, local markets are popping up all over the country and now farmers are supplying quality products at a great price directly from the farmhouse. This has many benefits as the products are fresh, often healthier, sometimes organic and always tastier. A wealth of artisan producers, such as the Blue Haven Food Company, are now also supplying the larger supermarkets and have also opened small stores all over Ireland. These are a great source of quality produce, readily available on the shelf. So remember to look out for our products next time you go shopping!

Remember, buying locally and seasonally when possible is always great value and good advice to follow.

Conversion Tables

Weight

Metric	Imperial
7g	¼ oz
10g	½ oz
25g	1 oz
50g	2 oz
75g	3 oz
110g	4 oz
150g	5 oz
175g	6 oz
200g	7 oz
225g	8 oz
250g	9 oz
275g	10 oz
310g	11 oz
350g	12 oz
380g	13 oz
400g	14 oz
425g	15 oz
450g	16 oz (1 lb)
700g	1½ lb
900g	2 lb
1kg	2½ lb
1.35kg	3 lb
2kg	4½ lb

Liquids:

Metric	Imperial	US Cups
15ml	½ fl oz	1 tbsp
30ml	1 fl oz	2 tbsp
55ml	2 fl oz	¼ cup
75ml	3 fl oz	⅜ cup
125ml	4 fl oz	½ cup
150ml	5 fl oz	⅔ cup
175ml	6 fl oz	¾ cup
250ml	8 fl oz	1 cup
275ml	10 fl oz	1¼ cups
570ml	1 pint	
1 litre	1¾ pints	4 cups

Note: a teaspoon is 5ml and a tablespoon 15ml, gently rounded.

Oven equivalent temperatures used:

°C	°F	Gas Mark
110	225	Gas ¼
140	275	Gas 1
150	300	Gas 2
170	325	Gas 3
180	350	Gas 4
190	375	Gas 5
200	400	Gas 6
220	425	Gas 7
230	450	Gas 8
240	475	Gas 9

There's nothing like a family Christmas! Everyone together from near and far, celebrating the season with a traditional Christmas dinner. Jon, James and I show you how you can make your Christmas Day perfect, with a menu, shopping list and recipes galore.

A Traditional
Christmas

❧ MENU ❧

Traditional Christmas Dinner

Smoked salmon with beet leaves and caper salsa (page 64)
Traditional garden vegetable soup (page 60)

❧ ❧ ❧ ❧ ❧

Perfect roast turkey (page 76)
Traditional honey roast ham (page 78)
Crispy roast potatoes (page 22)
Carrot and parsnip purée (page 22)
Brussel sprouts with chestnuts (page 22)

❧ ❧ ❧ ❧ ❧

Traditional Christmas pudding (page 130)
Mince pies (page 136)

SHOPPING LIST

400g smoked salmon
4 bunches of baby spinach
caper salsa (from your larder)
830g butter
10 carrots
4 parsnips
1 large onion
2 sticks of celery
3kg large potatoes
800ml vegetable stock
20ml cream
1 large turkey (already ordered,
just to collect)
4 slices of smoked bacon
1 handful of rosemary
1 handful of sage
thyme & garlic butter (from
your larder)
honey
Dijon mustard
English mustard
7 oranges
3 lemons
225g cooking apples (approx 4
apples)
450g brown sugar
600 - 750g Brussel sprouts
200g cooked chestnuts

1 handful flat parsley
1 tub goose fat
maple syrup
sea salt
cracked pepper
250g raisins
425g sultanas
250g glacé cherries
100g suet
rum
brandy
cinnamon
nutmeg
ground ginger
2 tbsp ground mixed spice
fresh ginger
60g ground almonds
25 g flaked almonds
140g breadcrumbs
2 eggs
sweet pastry - see page 136
100ml olive oil
2 tsp whole cloves
50g sugar
200g plain flour
110g currants
½ tsp ground cinnamon

Christmas Vegetables

Sage and onion stuffing *Serves 4*

1 tsp fresh sage, finely chopped
½ clove garlic, minced
200g onion, finely chopped
40g butter
1 tsp chopped chives
75g breadcrumbs
salt & pepper

1. Melt butter in a small pot. Add onions and cook over a low heat until soft.
2. Add the garlic and finely chopped sage. Cook for 1 minute and add breadcrumbs, chives and a pinch of salt and pepper.

Crispy roast potatoes

4 tbsp goose fat
2kg large potatoes - Maris Piper or King Edward

1. Pre-heat oven to 190°C/375°F/Gas 5.
2. Peel, wash and cut and quarter the potatoes. Bring a pot of water to the boil, add the potatoes and boil for about 8 minutes.
3. While they are cooking, put the goose fat in a roasting tray and put into the oven.
4. Strain the potatoes. While the potatoes are in the strainer give them a good shake to roughen up the edges - this will help them to crisp up. When the fat is hot, add the potatoes to the tray, and baste with the fat. Cook for a further 30 minutes. This can be done when the turkey is out of the oven and resting before carving.

Brussel sprouts with chestnuts

600g – 750g Brussel sprouts
30g butter
200g cooked chestnuts
2 tbsp chopped flat parsley

1. Bring a pot of water to the boil, add the sprouts and cook them for 10 minutes.
2. In a saucepan melt the butter, add the chestnuts and cook for 2 minutes.
3. Strain the sprouts and add them to the saucepan. Cook for a further 2 minutes, season to taste and sprinkle with chopped parsley.

Carrot and parsnip purée

4 carrots - peeled & roughly chopped
4 parsnips - peeled & roughly chopped
400g butter
3 tbsp double cream
2 tbsp maple syrup
sea salt & cracked black pepper

1. Boil the vegetables in salted water for 20 minutes, strain the water and leave them in the pot for a further 2 minutes to allow excess water to steam off.
2. Add the butter to the vegetables over a low heat.
3. Then, add the maple syrup and cook for a further minute.
4. Blitz the vegetables in a food processor, add salt & pepper to taste.
5. Finally, add the double cream and mix well.

It's easy to miss out on St Stephen's Day, treating it just as the day after Christmas, when the leftovers must be faced. But it can be much more than that – a festive and feasting occasion in itself. All it needs is a little imagination – or borrow ours! Just look at the fabulous recipes we have for you in this section!

St. Stephen's Day

❧ MENU ❧

St. Stephen's Day

Wild mushroom and chestnut soup (page 56)

Thai curry (page 88)

Seafood pie (page 98)

Fresh berry roulade (page 140)

SHOPPING LIST

1 shallot
1 bulb of garlic
200g butter
100g flour
600g wild mushrooms
1½ litres vegetable stock
¾ glass white wine
525ml cream
50g cooked chestnuts
4 chicken breasts
3 carrots
2 sticks of celery
1 courgette
1 red onion
1 red pepper
1 yellow pepper
100g curry paste (from your larder)
200ml coconut cream
fish sauce
½ red chilli
olive oil
600g mixed fish
500g potatoes
500ml fish stock
2 tbsp cornflour
4 eggs
250g caster sugar
125g strawberries
125g raspberries
30g dark chocolate
salt & pepper
1 onion

Children make Christmas. And what better way to enjoy your children and Christmas together than by letting them help you with the festive preparations– or even cook up some treats of their own!
We have put together some great ideas here for you!

Nana's

Cooking
with Kids

MENU

Kids' Menu

Gingerbread men (page 152)

Cupcakes (page 158)

Strawberry smoothie (page 156)

Strawberry shortbread with pastry cream (page 154)

SHOPPING LIST

350g unsalted butter
340g brown sugar
2 tbsp ground ginger
2 tsp ground cinnamon
3 tsp finely grated lemon zest
525g golden syrup
230g honey
13 eggs
1125g plain flour
2 tsp bicarbonate of soda
½ tsp salt
500g butter
350 ml cream
1 tsp baking powder
3 tbsp approx. vanilla essence
250g icing sugar
2tsp vanilla essence
500ml milk
28 strawberries
1 banana
½ pineapple
vanilla ice cream
orange juice
1 tbsp maple syrup
½ vanilla bean
100g granulated sugar
25g cornflour
50g castersugar

Do you remember making gingerbread men with your mom? Try it with your kids using our simple, but delicious, recipe!

The end of a year – and the start of a new one! Time to look back –
and to look forward, too. A gala New Year's Eve Dinner is a wonderful
way to celebrate in style – let us show you how.

New Year's Gala Dinner

❧ MENU ❧

New Year's Gala Dinner

Scallops with lemon and dill butter (page 68)
Curried parsnip soup (page 58)

Beef fillet with fondant potato (page 84)
Baked halibut with gruyère cheese (page 94)

Chocolate and chestnut marquise (page 142)

SHOPPING LIST

12 scallops
Lemon and dill butter (from
your larder)
2 lemons
fresh dill
800g butter
1 onion
8 parsnips
8 potatoes
1 litre vegetable stock
curry powder
600ml cream
olive oil
4 x 150g fillet steaks
garlic
380g halibut
gruyère cheese
8 spears of asparagus
7 eggs
165g caster sugar
200g 70% chocolate
65g cocoa powder
200ml chestnut purée
vanilla essence
salt & pepper
1 flat leaf of parsley
garlic butter (from your
larder)

38

Celebrating in style with a gala New Year's Eve Dinner means you need something more sophisticated than your usual bottle of plonk!
Here I share my favourite cocktails with you – you won't get much more sophisticated than this (or if you do, you won't be able to pronounce it!).

New Year's
Cocktails

MENU

New Year's Cocktail Party

Grandma Chow's crispy crab wontons (page 186)

New Year's Eve prawns and salsa (page 190)

Risotto balls (page 188)

Baby goats' cheese tarts (page 184)

Champagne cocktails (page 169)

Raspberry and chocolate-flavoured espresso
martini (page 166)

SHOPPING LIST

1 packet of wonton skins
fresh ginger
1 bulb of garlic
1 bunch of spring onions
sweet soy sauce
fresh coriander
4 eggs
150ml milk
16 tiger prawns
2 beef tomatoes
1 red chilli
4 limes
4 lemons
1 shallot
1 green pepper
150g cooked crab meat
salt & pepper
300g Arborio rice
200g flour
300g fresh breadcrumbs
12 cherry tomatoes
caster sugar

oregano leaves
olive oil
sea salt
cracked black pepper
325g puff pastry
150g Ardsallagh goat's
cheese
2 bottles of champagne
orange juice
peach purée
raspberry purée
40ml raspberry vodka
espresso
Tia Maria
icing sugar
good quality chocolate
aïoli (optional)
cranberry juice (optional)
sweet chilli sauce (optional)
plum sauce (optional)
sunflower oil – for frying

Christmas and New Year are always a time for indulgence. Forget the diet – just for a few days! Feast your eyes – and those of your family and guests – on Jon and James' delectably sinful temptations.

Heavenly
desserts

MENU

Dessert Buffet

Traditional Christmas pudding (page 130)

Tiramisu (page 132)

Mince pies (page 136)

Ferrero Rocher bombe (page 134)

Fresh berry roulade (page 140)

Pistachio truffles (page 146)

SHOPPING LIST

- 250g raisins
- 425g sultanas
- 250g glacé cherries
- 125g butter
- 450g brown sugar
- 200ml rum
- 1 tsp cinnamon
- ½ tsp nutmeg
- ½ tsp ground ginger
- 50g fresh ginger
- 60g ground almonds
- 140g breadcrumbs
- 18 eggs
- 500g mascarpone cheese
- 380g caster sugar
- 25 pieces of sponge fingers
- 120ml strong espresso coffee
- 60ml Kahlua liqueur
- 225g cooking apples
- 110g shredded suet

- 110g currants
- 5 oranges
- 3 lemons
- 25g flaked almonds
- 2 tsp mixed ground spice
- 6 tbsp brandy
- 300ml milk
- 1 leaf gelatine
- 3 tbsp water
- 50g sugar
- 200g plain flour
- 1005g dark chocolate
- 4 Fererro Rocher
- 845ml whipped cream
- 125g strawberries
- 125g raspberries
- 8 – 10 tbsp unsweetened cocoa
- salt
- 50g pistachio nuts

Start the New Year the right way – with a delicious brunch!
Never mind the calories – just enjoy the special dishes we have prepared
for you.

New Year's Day Brunch

MENU

New Year's Day Brunch

Eggs Benedict (my way!) (page 172)

Bloody Mary (page 166)

Pancakes (page 178)

Steak sandwich (page 180)

SHOPPING LIST

450g butter
1 tbsp white wine vinegar
8 slices of smoked streaky
bacon
10 eggs
8 slices of brioche or 4
english muffins halved
150g plain flour
1 tsp baking powder
½ tsp salt
2 tbsp caster sugar
150ml milk
2 tbsp butter
1 shot of vodka
380ml tomato juice
1 lemon
Worcestershire sauce
Tabasco sauce
celery
4 sirloin steaks -
approximately 180g - 200g
8 slices crusty white
bread
12 cherry tomatoes
rocket
1 onion
8 button mushrooms
olive oil
sea salt & cracked pepper
balsamic vinegar
3 cloves garlic, crushed

Women's Little Christmas marks the end of the festive season – an excuse for a party if I ever heard one! So here's our take on an easy-to-prepare

Women's Little Christmas

❧ MENU ❧

Women's Little Christmas

Mussels diablo (page 118)

Hummus (page 126)

Beef tomato and buffalo mozzarella salad (page 102)

Tempura vegetables (page 106)

Duck pancakes (page 66)

❧ ❧ ❧ ❧ ❧

Cranberry mojito (page 168)

Mulled wine (page 162)

SHOPPING LIST

1 kg mussels

basil leaves

garlic

1 tbsp red curry paste

olive oil

sea salt & cracked pepper

2 tsp fish sauce

250ml chicken stock

2 tins cooked chickpeas

2 lemons

100ml extra virgin olive oil

50g tahini paste

1 half roast duck, meat removed and shredded

12 Chinese pancakes

1 cucumber

8 spring onions

1 bottle of hoisin sauce

4 baby courgettes

2 sweet potatoes

4 baby leeks

1 parsnip

1 aubergine

sweet chilli sauce (optional)

sweet soy sauce (optional)

80g cornflour

80g self-raising flour

200ml sparkling water

salt & pepper

sunflower oil

beef tomatoes

buffalo mozzarella cheese

balsamic vinegar

10 mint leaves

2 sugar cubes

½ lime, cut into wedges

basil leaves

pesto

40ml white rum

100ml cranberry juice

cranberries

mint

1 bottle dry red wine

1 lemon

200ml orange juice

½ cup sugar

2 cinnamon sticks

4 - 5 whole cloves

½ tblsp nutmeg, grated

50 ml brandy

Sugar syrup

Recipes

Wild mushroom and chestnut soup

Serves 6

1 shallot, finely diced
2 cloves of garlic, finely diced
100g butter, cubed
100g flour
600g wild mushrooms
1½ litres vegetable stock – see page 195
salt & pepper
¼ glass white wine
100ml cream to finish
50g cooked chestnuts
Chestnut pesto - see page 198

1. Place three-quarters of the butter, the shallot and garlic into a pot and sweat off for about 2 minutes.
2. Add a third of the mushrooms and sweat for a further 2 minutes.
3. Remove the pot from the heat. Gradually add all of the flour, mixing well with a wooden spoon until you have almost a sandy texture.
4. Place the pot back on the heat and pour in the wine, bringing it back to the boil. Add the vegetable stock and keep stirring. Add a further one-third of the mushrooms and cook gently for a further 12 minutes, continually stirring the soup to avoid sticking. Add the cream and cook for a further minute or until it comes back to the boil.
5. While the soup is cooking, roughly chop the chestnuts, then sweat off the remaining mushrooms in a hot pan with the remaining butter for 3 minutes. Add the chestnuts and cook for 1 minute. Leave this to one side.
6. When the soup is cooked, blitz it in a food-processor or with a hand-held mixer until smooth. Add seasoning to taste.
7. To serve, simply pour soup into bowls. Then take a spoon of the mushroom and chestnut mix and place in the centre of the bowl and drizzle a little of the chestnut pesto over the soup.

"I love mushroom soup – simple but very rewarding."

Curried parsnip soup

Serves 6

100g butter
1 medium onion, chopped
8 large parsnips, peeled and finely chopped
2 large potatoes, peeled and diced
1 litre vegetable stock – see page 195
1 tbsp curry powder
200ml cream
salt & pepper
drizzle of olive oil

1. Place a large pot on a medium heat and melt the butter.
2. Gently cook the onions until softened.
3. Add parsnips and cook for a further few minutes.
4. Next, add in the curry powder and cook for a minute before adding the diced potato and the vegetable stock. Bring to the boil and simmer until all the ingredients are soft.
5. Then add the cream, bring back to the boil and purée the soup. Check taste and add salt and pepper as necessary.
6. Drizzle olive oil over the top and serve.

59

"This is a great winter warmer. The curry flavours marry well with parsnips. It's a perfect evening treat."

Traditional garden vegetable soup

serves 4

25g butter
6 carrots, peeled and finely chopped
1 large onion, peeled and chopped
2 sticks of celery, chopped
3 large potatoes, peeled and chopped
800ml vegetable stock – see page 195
100ml cream
salt & pepper

1. In a large pot, melt the butter and gently cook the carrots, onion and celery for 3 minutes.
2. Add the stock and potatoes, bring to the boil and cook for a further 12 minutes or until the vegetables are soft.
3. Add the cream and then bring back to the boil. Purée with a hand blender or, if using an upright blender, only fill to a third and cover with a tea towel.
4. Season and serve.

"A simple soup for any time of the year. Just use seasonal ingredients for maximum flavour."

Pumpkin and ginger soup

Serves 6 - 8

*2kg pumpkin flesh, skinned and
de-seeded and roughly chopped
1 large onion, finely diced
2 cloves of garlic, chopped
1 thumb-sized piece of ginger, grated
2 litres vegetable stock – see page 195
375ml coconut milk - optional
½ red chilli, seeds removed and sliced thinly
- optional
salt & pepper
olive oil*

1. Pre-heat the oven to 160°C/325°F/Gas 3.
2. Roast the roughly-chopped pumpkin in the oven for 20 minutes.
3. Meanwhile, add a drizzle of oil to a saucepan and sauté the onion until soft and translucent.
4. Add the ginger and garlic and cook for a further 2 minutes.
5. Add all the stock (or, if using coconut milk, add 1 litre) and bring to the boil, season lightly and simmer.
6. Remove the pumpkin flesh from the oven and add to the liquid and return to the boil (if using them, add the coconut milk and chilli now).
7. Use a liquidiser to blend the soup. Return to the pot, check the seasoning and serve.

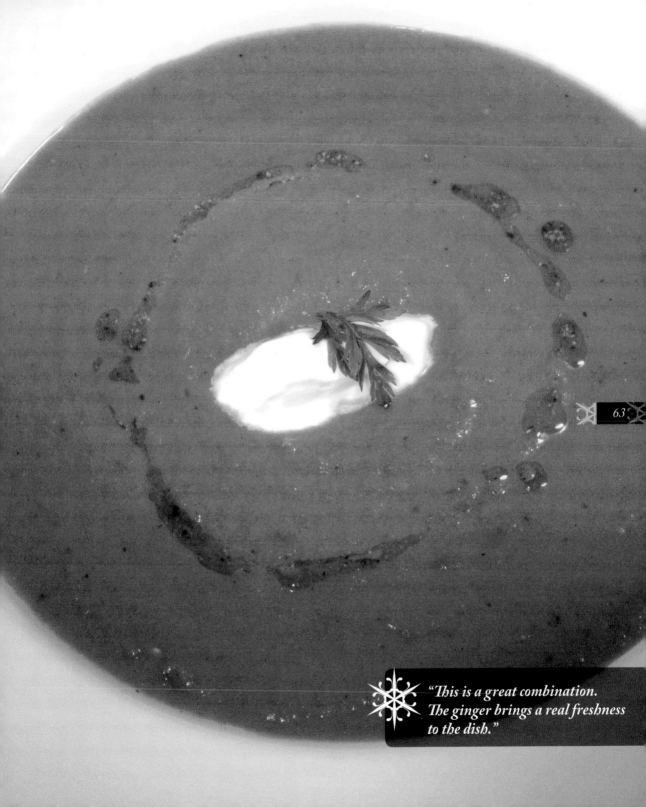

63

Smoked salmon with beet leaves

Single serving - increase accordingly.

100g sliced smoked salmon
1 bunch baby beet leaves - or baby spinach
1 tbsp caper salsa – see below

1. Arrange each slice of smoked salmon around the centre of the plate, slightly overlapping.
2. Line baby beet leaves along the centre of the smoked salmon.
3. Drizzle the dish with the vibrant caper salsa.

Caper salsa

250g parsley
15g anchovy fillets
10g capers
1 clove of garlic, chopped
½ tsp Dijon mustard
½ tsp vinegar
1 tbsp lemon juice
100ml olive oil

Blend all ingredients to a rough purée and refrigerate until needed (keeps for up to 3 weeks).

"The perfect Christmas starter
– light and flavourful."

Duck pancakes

Serves 4

½ roast duck, meat removed and shredded
12 Chinese pancakes – available at your
supermarket
1 cucumber
4 spring onions
1 bottle of hoisin sauce

1. Cut cucumber into 3, half each portion, remove the centre and slice thinly.
2. Cut the spring onions into half, then slice thinly.
3. Arrange each item in a separate bowl. Serve the duck, hoisin sauce and pancakes warm. Allow people to choose their own fillings, fill their pancakes and enjoy.

"A classic oriental dish, great for parties and sharing."

Scallops with lemon and dill butter

Serves 4

*12 scallops - make sure you get fresh scallops and
ask for the shells - you can use the shells to serve
them in*
*lemon and dill butter - see recipes for compound
butters on page 196*
1 lemon
some fresh dill
small knob of butter

1. To begin, clean the scallops. If you wish, remove the roe or ask your fishmonger to do so. Also make sure the fishmonger removes the sinew or muscle attaching the scallops to the shells. Then clean the shells and place in the oven 2 minutes before serving the dish.
2. Place a pan on a high heat. When the pan is just starting to smoke, put in the knob of butter and put the scallops into the pan. After about 1 minute, turn the scallops and cook for a further minute maximum.
3. Squeeze the juice from the lemon over the scallops. Remove from the pan and place onto kitchen paper to remove excess browned butter.
4. Take the now warm shells out of the oven. Place a scallop into each shell and then a sliver of lemon and dill butter over each scallop.
5. Serve 3 scallops per person and garnish with a sprig of dill.

Yep, it's that easy!

"With great products it's sometimes best to keep it simple"

Tiger prawn cocktail

Serves 4

*16 large tiger prawns – ask your fishmonger for
deveined prawns
2 beef tomatoes, roughly diced into small pieces,
about 1cm
½ red chilli, cut, de-seeded and finely chopped
2 limes
1 small shallot, finely diced
1 green pepper, finely diced
lime slices – to garnish*

1. To make the salsa, place the tomatoes, red chilli, shallot and green pepper into a bowl and squeeze the juice of the limes over it all. Cover and put into a fridge for at least 4 hours.

2. Bring a pot of water to the boil, season, and add in the prawns. When the water comes back up to the boil, remove from the heat and place under the tap with cold running water. Leave until fully cooled. Remove and drain the prawns and place in the fridge until required.

3. To serve, you will need 4 martini glasses half-filled with crushed ice. Next, place a thin slice of lime on the ice. On this slice, place a tablespoon of the salsa. Then arrange the prawns 4 per glass, so the tail of each prawn hangs over the edge of the glass.

"*Looks class, tastes class!*"

Beef and baby pear salad with hazelnut dressing

Serves 4

Dressing

2 tbsp crushed hazelnuts
2 tbsp balsamic vinegar
6 tbsp olive oil
a little sea salt & cracked black pepper

Mix all of the above ingredients and leave to blend for a couple of hours at room temperature.

Salad

4 handfuls of mixed seasonal leaves, washed
half a handful of flat leaf parsley
1 red shallot, finely diced
1 red pepper, cut into thin strips
3 tbsp lightly roasted pine nuts
parmesan cheese
350g fillet of beef strips*
1 small pear, peeled and cut into very thin slices

1. Place the leaves, parsley, shallot, pepper slices, pine nuts, pear slices and three-quarters of the dressing in a large bowl and mix gently together. Divide the salad on to 4 plates.
2. Place the pan on a high heat, drizzle with a little olive oil. When starting to smoke, add the beef. Cook for about 2 minutes. At the last minute, add the remaining dressing to the pan. Season with a little salt and serve with the salad.
3. A nice touch is to shave a little parmesan over the salad.

* For this recipe, ask your butcher for trimmed fillet tails. This is the tail end piece of a fillet of beef but you should be able to get it for half the price of fillet steak. Ask the butcher to cut it into strips for you. A good butcher will cut across the fillet, ensuring the meat remains tender.

The centrepiece of a traditional Christmas dinner – and some modern alternatives.

Meat
and fish

Perfect roast turkey

2 slices of thyme and garlic butter –
see page 196
4 slices of smoked bacon chopped
1 turkey
a handful of rosemary and sage
salt & pepper
a good measure of olive oil

1. Pre-heat the oven to 200°C/400°F/Gas 6. Work your hand between the turkey breast and the skin to create a pocket.
2. Next, mix the smoked bacon with thyme and garlic butter and place in the pocket.
3. Fill the cavity with rosemary and sage. Next, season the bird inside and out with the oil, salt and pepper.
4. Place in the oven and use the guide below to gauge times. Remember to baste the turkey every 30 minutes as it cooks.

Cooking times

The following is an approximate gauge for cooking whole turkeys. As a rule allow a pound weight per person when trying to gauge what size turkey to buy.

To cook an unstuffed turkey as above, allow the
following:
6 - 8 pounds (2.5 - 3.5 kg) 2.5 - 3 hours
8 - 12 pounds (3.5 - 5.5 kg) 3 - 4 hours
12 - 16 pounds (5.5 - 7.5 kg) 4 - hours
16 - 20 pounds (7.5 - 9 kg) 5 - 5.5 hours
For stuffed turkeys add 30 minutes to your
cooking time

I usually cover the turkey for the middle section of the cooking time, then remove the covering for the last 30 minutes.

PLEASE REMEMBER THAT TURKEYS AND OVENS ARE ALL DIFFERENT, SO USE A PROBE TO ENSURE THE TURKEY REACHES 80°C.

Traditional honey roast ham

Honey glaze

4 tbsp runny honey
2 tbsp Dijon mustard
2 tbsp English mustard
2 oranges – juice only
2 tbsp brown sugar
2 tsp whole cloves

1. Pre-heat the oven to 230°C/450°F/Gas 8.
2. While the oven is heating, combine the ingredients above in a saucepan and slowly melt over a low heat.
3. Remove the skin of the ham. Then take a sharp knife and score the fat, creating a criss-cross diamond pattern on the surface / fat of the cooked ham. Try not to penetrate the meat itself, just the fat.
4. Stud the meat with the cloves in the centre of each diamond.
5. Next, generously brush the ham with the glaze and bake in the oven for approximately 12 minutes, checking that it's not burning. If the ham is not fully glazed re-brush and put back for a further 2 to 3 minutes.
6. Remove and leave to cool.

However, if you are planning to cook a ham on the bone, allow 500g uncooked weight per person (maximum) - you will find this is more than enough. Allow 22 to 26 minutes per 500g cooking time.

This always looks amazing when placed in the centre of the table and carved. And it also works a treat as a midnight snack, either on its own or in a sandwich. My favourite is with some sautéed left-over roast potatoes.

79

"Christmas is that rare occasion where there is a reason to buy and cook a whole ham. There are two ways to do this: you can buy a raw ham on the bone or alternatively what I recommend you do is buy a cooked ham on the bone from your local butcher. Personally, I use the Chicken Inn in the English Market in Cork - their hams are always perfectly cooked and always top quality."

Kassler bacon with creamy red pepper sauce

Serves 4

800g Kassler bacon - from O'Flynns in Cork,
if you can possibly do so - they're class!
2 red peppers, diced approx. 1cm
1 shallot, finely diced
2 cloves garlic, finely diced
300ml cream
½ glass white wine
creamy mash for 4 - see below
carrot & parsnip purée - see page 22
olive oil

1. Pre-heat oven to 180°C/350°F/Gas 4.
2. Cut the bacon into 4 pieces. Place on a hot tray and into the oven. This will cook in about 18 minutes, so turn them after 9 minutes.
3. While the bacon is cooking, heat another pan. To make the sauce, add in a drizzle of olive oil and then add the shallot, garlic and peppers. Cook for 3 to 4 minutes.
4. Then add the wine and reduce by half. Next, add the cream. Bring to the boil and turn down the heat and cook slowly for approximately 10 minutes.
5. When the bacon is cooked, pour the juice into the sauce and leave it to rest for 2 minutes. While the meat is resting, stir and taste the sauce and then season.
6. To plate, place a scoop of mash into the centre of the plate and place the bacon on top. Spoon the sauce over the dish and serve with carrot and parsnip purée on the side.

Mashed potato (quick & easy)

900g Maris Pipers or Desirée potatoes
50g butter
4 tbsp milk
4 tbsp double cream
salt & pepper

1. Wash, peel and rewash the potatoes. Cut them into fairly small even pieces.
2. Bring a pot of water to the boil and boil for 20 minutes. Strain and leave to one side for 4 minutes to allow any excess water to evaporate. Melt the butter in a saucepan on a low heat, add the milk, then add the potatoes and mash.
3. Add the cream and salt & pepper to taste and mix well.

"A simple but really pleasing dish."

81

Spiced beef

Serves 8 - 10

I like to cook the spiced beef the day before in a large pot of water with a handful of bay leaves.

1. Based on a 2.5kg piece of corned beef, cook for about 30 minutes at a rolling boil. Reduce heat to medium-low so that the water is at a gentle boil, cover, and cook for 3½ hours.
2. Allow to cool in the cooking liquor as it dries out otherwise.

I love to serve this with parsley sauce - see below - and vegetables. Enjoy.

Parsley sauce

400ml milk
20g butter
20g plain flour
20g flat leaf parsley
20g chopped flat leaf parsley
1 bay leaf
1 tsp black peppercorns
1 shallot - peeled & sliced
salt & pepper

1. Place the milk, the un-chopped parsley, bay leaf, peppercorns and the shallot into a saucepan and bring to the boil. When the milk is bubbling well at the sides, remove from the heat and strain the milk into a container.
2. Next, place another saucepan on the heat and melt the butter at a low heat. Add the flour and mix well, then turn the heat back up and whisk in the milk slowly, stirring continuously. When the mixture is thick, glossy and shiny - after about 8 minutes - add the chopped parsley, season to taste and serve.

"Old fashioned, but an absolute necessity with spiced beef"

"A Cork tradition and a wonderful addition to the Christmas table."

Beef fillet with fondant potato

Serves 4

4 x 150g fillet steaks
4 medium potatoes
400g butter
1 clove of garlic
flat leaf parsley
garlic butter – see page 196

1. Pre-heat the oven to 180°C/350°F/Gas 4. Grease an ovenproof dish.
2. For the fondant potatoes, peel the potato and cut into thin slices.
3. Put a small oven-proof dish on the stove to heat and melt the butter. Then add the garlic and cook for 1 minute. Place the potatoes in the dish and brown one side in the oven for 30 minutes, then take out and turn the potatoes over and cook for another 30 minutes.
4. Heat a griddle pan (if you do not have a griddle, use a frying pan), and fry the fillets for 3 minutes on each side. Ideally, the fillets should be eaten medium to rare. When all the fillets are done, place them in the oven for 5 minutes, remove and let them rest for 2 minutes.
5. Serve the fillets garnished with the parsley, the fondant potatoes and a small knob of garlic butter.

85

Classic beef stroganoff

Serves 4

700g beef, ideally fillet, cut into thin slices
1 large onion
2 large cloves of garlic
20 button mushrooms
6 medium gherkins
150ml cream
4 tbsp sour cream
drizzle of olive oil
salt & pepper

1. Heat the olive oil in a large saucepan and brown off the beef pieces. When done, put the beef to the side.
2. In the same pan, sauté the garlic, onion and mushrooms until soft.
3. Slice the gherkins and add to the pan and cook for a couple of minutes. Salt and pepper to taste.
4. Now put the beef pieces back in the pan and cook for 3 to 4 minutes.
5. Pour in the cream and reduce until the sauce has become slightly thicker than the consistency of double cream.
6. Finally, add sour cream and mix well. Traditionally, beef stroganoff is served with long grain rice.

"Easy, hearty and tasty!"

Thai curry

Serves 4

4 chicken breasts, cut into pieces
1 large carrot, thinly sliced
1 large courgette, thinly sliced
1 medium red onion, thinly sliced
1 red pepper, thinly sliced
1 yellow pepper, thinly sliced
100g curry paste – see recipe on page 200
200ml coconut cream
salt and pepper
1 tsp fish sauce
½ red chilli, finely sliced
olive oil – for frying

1. Get a pan really hot, add the oil, then brown off the chicken pieces and put to one side.
2. Add all the other vegetables except the courgettes and fry in the pan for 5 minutes.
3. Add the curry paste and cook for 2 minutes.
4. Add the coconut cream and cook for 5 minutes. Add the courgettes and cook for 2 more minutes.
5. Add the chilli and fish sauce. Taste and add seasoning, if needed. Serve with long grain rice.

Salmon en papillote

Serves 4

4 x 150g pieces of salmon
200ml white wine
400g baby potatoes, thinly sliced
4 bay leaves
1 fennel bulb, thinly sliced
2 carrots, very thinly sliced
salt & pepper

1. Preheat the oven to 180°C/350°F/Gas 4.
2. Cut 4 large squares of tin-foil and place on a table. Place a piece of salmon in the centre of each and raise all four corners of the foil.
3. Divide the wine, bay leaves, fennel, carrot and potatoes into each parcel. Add a little seasoning and seal parcels closed so all the ingredients and the liquid are trapped inside. Cook for 15 minutes and serve.

Oven-baked cod with 3 tomato ragout

Serves 4

4 large pieces of cod (about 220g–240g each)
½ glass white wine
50g tomato paste
100g sundried tomatoes
4 large beef tomatoes, roughly chopped
1 tin chopped tomatoes
200g cherry tomatoes
1 large courgette, cut into 3cm diced pieces
1 clove of garlic, finely chopped
1 tbsp balsamic vinegar
2 tbsp sugar
salt & pepper
olive oil
butter

1. Pre-heat the oven to 180°C/350°F/Gas 4.
2. Heat the butter in an oven tray and place the cod on it skin-side down, season well and place in the oven. Cooking will depend on the thickness of the cod but 8 minutes is about average. If it's very thin, check the fish after 6 minutes; if thicker the fish may need longer.
3. Next, put a pot on to high heat and add a generous drizzle of olive oil. Add the sundried tomatoes, cherry tomatoes, beef tomatoes, garlic and courgette pieces and the sugar and sweat for about 2 minutes. Then add the tomato paste and cook for a further 2 minutes.
4. Add the wine and cook for a further 2 minutes. Add the tin of chopped tomatoes and balsamic vinegar and cook for a further 2 minutes.
5. Remove from the heat and season to taste.
6. To plate, place a generous amount of the ragout into the centre of a pasta bowl. On this, place a portion of cod skin-side up. Add a little more of the juice from the ragout if required.

Enjoy!

"A lovely bistro-style dish - warming and filling".

Baked halibut with gruyère cheese

Serves 2

380g fresh halibut cut in two - your fishmonger
will do this
2 large potatoes
gruyère cheese, for grating
8 asparagus spears
30g butter
salt & pepper
1 lemon
olive oil

1. Pre-heat the oven to 170°C/325°F/Gas 3.
2. Boil the potatoes until cooked, set aside and then dice.
3. Heat a pan to medium heat, add the oil and place the fish skin-side down; this will ensure a nice crispy skin when fully cooked. Fry for a couple of minutes and transfer to a roasting tray and put into the oven to bake for 8 to 10 minutes, depending on the type of oven.
4. Drop the asparagus into boiling water for 30 seconds and remove. If not using immediately, cool with cold water to stop cooking.
5. Now place the potatoes and asparagus on a metal tray with a few small knobs of butter. Season and put under a grill on high until the asparagus is cooked, about 3-4 minutes.
6. When the halibut is done, remove and grate a generous amount of gruyère cheese over it, cover it and grill until the cheese is melted and almost bubbling.
7. Squeeze the lemon juice into the butter from the cooked asparagus and drizzle over the dish. Serve with the asparagus and potatoes and garnish with sliced lemon.

Quick yet delicious!

Prawn and courgette linguini

Serves 4

20 large tiger prawns
2 courgettes – chopped into 2cm chunks
½ glass dry white wine
300ml double cream
linguini pasta
20g parmesan cheese, freshly grated
olive oil – for frying
salt & pepper

1. Begin by cooking the pasta in boiling salted water and cook until it's *al dente* – that is until it retains a little bite. Remove and strain, place in a tray and drizzle with some olive oil and toss – this will stop the pasta from sticking together. Set this aside.
2. Heat some oil in a pan until almost smoking and add the tiger prawns, cook for 3 to 4 minutes, shaking the pan to cook the prawns evenly. Add in the courgettes, season and cook for a further 2 minutes.
3. Add the wine and reduce by half, then add the cream.
4. Bring to the boil and toss in the pasta and stir to coat it.
5. Finally, sprinkle over the cheese and serve in large bowls with chunks of crusty ciabatta.

Enjoy!

Seafood pie

Serves 4

600g mixed fish – cod, salmon, clams, prawns
and smoked haddock
1 onion, finely chopped
½ glass dry white wine
2 carrots, finely chopped
2 celery sticks, finely chopped
500g potatoes, peeled and washed
100g butter
50ml cream
2 tbsp cornflour
500ml fish stock – see page 195

1. Put a saucepan on the heat with a little olive oil. When hot add the clams to the oil and cook for about 2 minutes, then remove them from the pan and leave them to cool.
2. Bring a pot of water to the boil. Add a little salt to the boiling water and turn down the heat a little. Add the cod and the salmon, and after 1 minute add the smoked haddock. After 30 seconds add the shelled prawns and immediately remove the pan from the heat to rest for 1 minute. Then strain. Remove the clams from their shells, add to the rest of the seafood mixture and leave to rest.
3. In a large pot of salted water, put the potatoes on to boil.
4. Melt half of the butter in a large pot and cook onions until soft but not browned. Add the carrots and celery and cook for a further 5 minutes.
5. Add the wine and cook until only a syrup remains. Then add the fish stock and bring to the boil. Reduce heat and simmer for 10 minutes.
6. Add in the cream, return the pot to the boil. Then dissolve the cornflour in a little water and add to the pot, stirring continuously until thick. Reduce heat and leave to simmer.
7. Strain the potatoes when cooked and mash with the remaining butter and a pinch of salt and pepper and put to one side.
8. To construct the pie, pour the cooked warm fish into the dish, then pour over the creamy mix with the vegetables. Pipe the mashed potato on top or smooth with a spatula. Brush the top with a little melted butter and place under the grill on the middle shelf, until the potato is golden in colour and serve.

"The thing to remember when cooking fish is that it cooks very quickly, so please trust the recipe!"

A different kind of Christmas celebration.

Vegetarian Alternatives

Beef tomato and buffalo mozzarella salad

Single serving – increase accordingly.

beef tomatoes* – 1 per person
buffalo mozzarella** balls – 2 per 3 people
fresh basil leaves – as many as you like
cracked black pepper
pesto
balsamic vinegar

1. Slice the beef tomatoes into thin slices, about 1cm thick (discard top and bottom slices).
2. Slice the mozzarella into roughly the same size slices.
3. Overlap the tomato and cheese slices to create a circle on a plate.
4. Next, tear the basil leaves over the food. Drizzle with balsamic vinegar.
5. Lightly sprinkle with black pepper and drizzle with pesto.

Simple, sexy, tasty!

* Go to your local greengrocer and ask for beef tomatoes – proper juicy delicious beef tomatoes.
**Make sure it is buffalo mozzarella.

❄ *"This is a simple, stylish and yet one of the best starters you can serve."*

Vegetable cannelloni

Serves 4

12 lasagne sheets – fresh, if possible
1 bag of baby spinach
10 asparagus spears
5 roasted red peppers
120g feta cheese
500ml cream
50g Boursin garlic and herb cheese
1 tbsp olive oil
salt & pepper

1. Pre-heat the oven to 170°C/325°F/Gas 3.
2. Roughly chop the peppers, asparagus and spinach, cook on a low heat with the olive oil in a pot for about 10 minutes.
3. Place the fresh lasagne sheets in a pot of boiling water to soften them, remove and, after 5 minutes, lay out on a clean surface.
4. Place some of the pepper, asparagus and spinach mix, along with some feta cheese, onto each sheet and then roll the lasagne sheets tight enough to hold. Once the 12 sheets are rolled, place all the cannelloni tubes into an earthenware or Pyrex oven dish, pour all the cream over and crumble the Boursin cheese evenly over each tube. Season to taste.
5. Cover with foil and bake for 15 minutes.
6. To serve, just spoon onto a large plate and add a bowl of crispy garlic bread to the table for that finishing touch. Delicious!

Tempura vegetables

Serves 4 - 6

A selection of vegetables - 4 spring onions, 4 baby courgettes, 2 sweet potatoes, 4 baby leeks, 1 parsnip, 1 aubergine, etc.
sweet chilli sauce - optional
sweet soy sauce - optional

For the tempura batter:
80g cornflour - plus a little extra for dusting the vegetables
80g self-raising flour
200ml sparkling water – or even 7-Up
salt & pepper – for seasoning
sunflower oil – for frying

1. First, prepare the vegetables. Use the baby leeks, spring onion and baby courgettes as they are. Cut the rest into wedges roughly the size of your thumb. Before you fry the vegetables, lay out the ingredients.
2. Pour the oil into a deep saucepan and place on a high heat (you can use a deep fat fryer instead).
3. While it's heating, mix all of the tempura batter ingredients together and whisk well to a smooth mix. Have a tray with kitchen paper ready and a bowl with the extra cornflour in it.
4. Heat the oil to a medium heat. Dust the vegetables in the cornflour and dip into the batter mix quickly. Then place them into the hot oil (no more than a half dozen pieces at a time). Turn the vegetables in the oil, ensuring an even colour - this should take no more than 2 minutes.
5. Remove from the oil on to kitchen paper. Drain excess oil. Place onto a serving plate and serve with a dipping sauce - maybe a sweet chilli sauce or a sweet soy sauce (regular soy sauce can be a bit too salty).

"Easy, fun to cook and a great way to get your family to eat vegetables."

Twice-cooked spinach and cheese soufflé

Serves 4

50g butter
50g plain flour
275ml hot milk
50g spinach
100g good quality cheddar cheese
½ tsp smoked paprika
4 eggs, separated
100ml cream
40g grated parmesan cheese
salt & pepper

1. Preheat the oven to 180°C/350°F/Gas 4.
2. Butter 4 x 250ml ramekin dishes.
3. Cook spinach in a hot pan for about 1 minute. Cool, remove and chop finely.
4. Melt the butter in a pot over a low heat until foaming. Remove from the heat, then stir in the flour until well combined. Return pan on a medium-low heat and stir constantly for 1 minute until it is a smooth paste.
5. Gradually add the hot milk to the flour and butter mixture, stirring constantly for about 2 minutes, until smooth. Bring to the boil, then pour into a large bowl.
6. Add the cheddar cheese, paprika and spinach, then season with salt and pepper and stir until smooth.
7. Whisk in the egg yolks one at a time. In a separate bowl, whisk the egg whites to soft peaks. Gently fold one-third of the egg whites into the cheese mixture. Gently fold in another third of the egg whites, then finally fold in the remainder.
8. Three-quarter fill each ramekin. Place in a deep tray filled with enough boiling water to come halfway up the sides of the ramekins.
9. Bake in the oven for 20 minutes or until golden and risen, then remove from the oven and cool.
10. Just before serving, increase the oven to 220°C/425°F/Gas 7. Pour about 1 tablespoon of cream over the top of each one, scatter with parmesan, and bake for 8 to 10 minutes until the cheese is golden and the cream is bubbling. Serve immediately.

"A lovely starter to make ahead of time."

Wild mushroom risotto

Serves 4

500g Arborio rice
1½ litres vegetable stock – see page 195
50g butter
salt and pepper
200g wild mushrooms
truffle oil - optional but delicious
100g parmesan cheese
50ml mushroom stock – see page 195
100ml cream

1. Melt the butter in a saucepan and add the Arborio rice, toss and coat fully in the butter.
2. Add 350ml of the vegetable stock, cover and simmer until the stock has been absorbed. Then add another 350ml, continue this process until all of the stock has been absorbed by the rice and the rice is fully cooked. You may need more stock if the rice is not cooked enough – the rice should have a little bite to it – don't cook the rice until it's completely soft.
3. Now sauté the mushrooms in a wide saucepan until nearly soft, quickly add the Arborio rice and mix thoroughly. Now add a couple of ladles of mushroom stock and cook until absorbed. When ready, add the cream and parmesan cheese and cook for a few minutes until ready to serve.
4. Quickly spoon into a warm bowl and garnish either with a sprinkle of parmesan or a little dash of the truffle oil. Enjoy!

Puy lentil-stuffed aubergines on Tuscan-style vegetables

Serves 2

1 large aubergine	1 small leek
1 red pepper	80g Puy lentils
1 green pepper	25g butter
2 yellow peppers	20g tomato paste
1 courgette	580ml vegetable stock – see page195
1 clove of garlic	dash of red wine
25g parmesan cheese	salt & pepper

1. Pre-heat the oven to 180ºC/350ºF/Gas 4.
2. Soak the puy lentils for at least 1½ hours to soften and ensure they cook properly.
3. Cut the aubergine in two lengthways and place on a tray, skin-side down. Score the flesh with a knife almost to the bottom of the aubergine (without piercing the skin) from top-to-bottom and side-to-side 3 or 4 times. This will make it easier to remove the centre of the aubergine when stuffing it. Now sprinkle a little salt over the flesh and leave, to draw some of the moisture out while the lentils are soaking. When the lentils are ready, place the aubergine in the oven for 15 minutes.
4. Place the butter in a wide pot. Roughly chop the garlic and leek and add to the pot. Cook on a medium heat and stir for 5 minutes.
5. Add the lentils and cover with the stock. Cook for 20 minutes over a low heat. When the lentils have softened, add the cheese and season. Now cover with a lid and place to the side.
6. For the Tuscan vegetables, just cut them all into rough pieces, place in an oven tray with the tomato paste and wine and roast until soft. Scrape out the flesh of the cooked aubergine, chop and add it to the lentils and stir.
7. Now spoon this mix back into the aubergine and bake for a further 5 minutes.
8. To serve, spoon the Tuscan vegetables into a bowl and place the aubergine on top.

While this recipe takes some time, it is definitely worth it!

113

Sticking to the straight and narrow needn't be boring.

Healthier
options

Smoked mackerel and watercress salad

Serves 2

300g smoked mackerel
½ medium onion, finely diced
50g toasted pumpkin seeds
250g watercress, washed
1 Granny Smith apple, diced
2 tbsp cider vinegar
8 tbsp olive oil
25g walnut halves
salt & pepper

1 Check the mackerel for bones and remove.
2 Then combine all the ingredients in a large bowl, add vinegar and olive oil, then toss gently.
3 Season with salt and pepper. Then serve.

"A beautiful light dish. Lovely, peppery watercress is delicious with mackerel."

Mussels diablo (Devilled mussels)

Serves 2 - 4

1kg mussels*
couple of handfuls of basil leaves, finely
chopped
1 clove of garlic, finely chopped
1 tbsp red curry paste – see page 200
olive oil
sea salt
cracked pepper
2 tsp fish sauce
250ml chicken stock – see page 195

1. Heat a wok on a high flame / heat. When it begins to smoke, add the oil, garlic and the curry paste. Cook for about 1 minute.
2. Add the stock and the mussels, cover and cook for approximately 2 minutes more.
3. Add the fish sauce, stir and cook for 1 minute.
4. Add the basil leaves, pour into a bowl and serve. Add salt & pepper to taste.

This is a great sharing dish for a group with a bottle of "Corona" beer or just to fill a gap between meals. You can do a smaller portion as a starter or serve it as a main course with a little focaccia bread (see page 203) to mop up the juices.

* Get your fishmonger to wash and de-beard the mussels. Also, when you're washing them just before use, tap the mussels off the counter; any that don't close, discard.

"A bottle of Corona with a wedge of lime, spicy mussels, a roaring fire, good company - nuff said."

Sweet potato and lavender soup

Serves 4

2 tbsp olive oil
1 onion, roughly chopped
2 garlic cloves, crushed
¼ tsp chilli powder
600g sweet potato, peeled, diced
500g carrots, peeled, thinly sliced
2 tbsp lavender honey
300g can cooked chickpeas, drained, rinsed
½ small lemon, juiced
lavender flowers to decorate - dried is ok
800ml vegetable stock – see page 195
salt & pepper

1. Heat oil in a large saucepan over medium-high heat. Add the onion and garlic. Cook, stirring often, for 3 minutes.
2. Add the chilli powder. Cook, stirring, for 1 minute.
3. Add the sweet potato and carrot. Continue stirring for 5 minutes. Add the lavender honey and cook for 1 minute more.
4. Add the vegetable stock. Cover. Bring to the boil. Reduce heat to medium-low and simmer, stirring occasionally, for 20 minutes.
5. Add the chickpeas to the soup and simmer, covered, for 10 minutes or until the chickpeas are tender.
6. Blend soup, in batches, until smooth. Return to the saucepan over a low heat. Season with salt and pepper. Add lemon juice, stirring until hot (do not boil). Pour into bowls. Top with lavender flowers and serve.

121

"*Although unusual, used sparingly the lavender honey is a great background flavour. You will be pleasantly surprised.*"

Smoked chicken salad

Serves 4

4 breasts of smoked chicken
1 large eating apple, diced in 1cm pieces
hazelnut oil
balsamic vinegar
1 handful of chopped flat leaf parsley
4 handfuls of mixed baby leaves
sea salt & cracked black pepper

1. Cut each chicken breast into very thin slices, around 10 slices per breast. Fan a breast in a circular pattern around the edge of each plate.
2. Next, place the leaves, apple and parsley into a bowl.
3. Add a drizzle of the hazelnut oil and of the balsamic - be generous with both. Sprinkle with sea salt and cracked black pepper and mix well. Arrange in the centre of each plate. Serve & enjoy.

"A light, simple dish, easy to prepare – and a great detox dish over the holiday period."

Tomato and bean cassoulet

Serves 4

1 tin of cooked chickpeas
1 tin of cooked butter beans
3 tins of chopped tomatoes
1 onion, chopped
2 cloves of garlic, crushed
2 tsp cumin
2 tsp paprika
1 handful of basil leaves
olive oil
salt & pepper

1. Sauté the onion in a little olive oil until soft.
2. Add cumin and paprika and cook for 1 minute.
3. Add the tomatoes and garlic and cook over a medium heat for 10 minutes. Season with salt and pepper.
4. Add the beans and the chickpeas and bring to the boil.
5. Remove from the heat, add olive oil to taste and basil leaves. Mix lightly and serve.

125

"A really nice vegetarian option."

Hummus

2 tins of cooked chickpeas
5 cloves of garlic, finely chopped
2 lemons, zest and juice
100ml extra virgin olive oil
50g tahini paste

1. Wash the chickpeas in cold water. Drain and add the rest of the ingredients.
2. Blend in a food-processor until smooth. Check seasoning and adjust if necessary.

This is made to my taste but can be adapted to suit anyone's palate.

"A staple in my fridge. Gorgeous with warm pitta bread."

I can resist everything except temptation!

Heavenly desserts

Traditional Christmas pudding

Serves 4

250g raisins
250g sultanas
250g glacé cherries
zest of 4 oranges
zest of 2 lemons
250g butter
275g brown sugar
200ml rum
½ tsp cinnamon
½ tsp nutmeg
½ tsp ground ginger
50g fresh ginger, grated
60g ground almonds
140g breadcrumbs
4 eggs, beaten

1. Combine all the dry ingredients in a large mixing bowl, add eggs and mix well. Place in a 4lb pudding bowl, cover with greaseproof paper and tie with string.
2. Place lid on and cook in a pot of simmering water for 3 hours before removing. The pudding can be kept for be kept for up to 3 months, once it is stored in an air-tight container.

For a dessert buffet, take the same recipe and divide the mixture into smaller ½ pound pudding bowls and simmer in water for an hour less.

"A Christmas tradition."

Tiramisu

Serves 4

> *500g mascarpone cheese*
> *5 eggs, separated*
> *120g caster sugar – reserve 30g for the coffee*
> *25 sponge fingers*
> *120ml strong espresso coffee*
> *60ml Kahlua liqueur*

1. Beat the mascarpone until smooth. In a separate bowl, beat the egg yolks with 90g of the sugar until mixture is pale and fluffy. Gradually mix in softened mascarpone.
2. Using an electric mixer, whisk the egg whites until they form soft peaks. Fold into the mascarpone mix.
3. Line a large serving dish with half the sponge fingers.
4. Add the remaining sugar to the coffee and liqueur and drizzle over the sponge, which should be moist, not saturated.
5. Cover with half the egg mix, then repeat the process. Chill for at least an hour. Sprinkle with cocoa powder before serving.

To make mini tiramisus for a dessert buffet, follow the above recipe all the way and then use a dessert spoon to fill espresso cups to just below the top with the finished tiramisu. Pipe a little whipped cream over the top. Sprinkle with cocoa powder and serve in the saucer with a boudoir biscuit on the side.

"A nice Italian dessert "

Ferrero Rocher bombe

Serves 4

3 eggs
1 tsp caster sugar
300ml milk
1 leaf gelatine, soaked in cold water
3 tbsp water
300ml single cream
225g dark chocolate – for folding into the egg
custard
150g melted dark chocolate – min 60 % cocoa
solid, for coating the bombe
4 Ferrero Rocher chocolates

1. Separate the eggs, keeping the whites in a separate bowl. Place the egg yolks and sugar in a bowl and mix well.
2. Pour the milk into a saucepan and heat gently until almost boiling. Pour the hot milk on to the egg yolks, whisking until combined to make the custard.
3. Place the bowl over a pot of simmering water and stir until the mixture coats the back of a spoon. Drop in the gelatine and stir until combined.
4. Whip the cream until it is just holding its shape. Fold into the egg custard. Then melt the chocolate and fold in.
5. Place the mousse in a small lined loaf tin and push in the *Ferrero Rocher* sweets. Allow to set in a fridge. Remove and cut into four, ensuring a *Ferrero Rocher* sweet is in the centre of each piece. Place on a cold surface and coat with melted chocolate.
6. Return to the fridge. Remove 10 minutes before serving.

Mince pies

sweet pastry – see recipe below

1 egg, beaten for eggwash

mincemeat – see recipe below

caster sugar for dusting

1. Pre-heat the oven to 180°C/350°F/Gas 4.
2. Take a quantity of sweet pastry to suit the number of pies you're making and roll to about 1.5 cm thick. Then cut two discs for each pie, one slightly smaller than the other.
3. Butter a muffin tray and use the larger disc to make the base of the pie, then fill with mincemeat to three-quarters-full. Then eggwash the pastry around the mincemeat and cover with the top.
4. When finished all the pies, eggwash the tops and place in a pre-heated oven for 10 to 15 minutes or until beautifully golden on top. Remove from oven, place on a wire rack and dust with caster sugar.

Sweet pastry *Makes 12 pies*

1 whole egg

50g sugar

125g butter

200g plain flour

pinch of salt

1. Combine all the dry ingredients in a bowl.
2. Mix the eggs and add to the dry ingredients. Knead for 3 to 4 minutes. Wrap and refrigerate for 30 minutes before using.

Christmas mincemeat

225g cooking apples, cored and chopped

110g shredded suet

175g sultanas

110g currants

175g. soft dark brown sugar

1 orange, grated zest and juice

1 lemon, grated zest and juice

25g flaked almonds

2 tsp mixed ground spice

½ tsp ground cinnamon

6 tbsp brandy

Combine all the ingredients in a large mixing bowl and mix well. Place in sterilised jars and seal. This can be kept for up to 3 months.

Layered chocolate mousse

Serves 6 – 8

3 eggs
1 tbsp caster sugar
300ml milk
1 leaf of gelatine, soaked in 3 tbsp cold water
300ml cream
75g dark chocolate
75g white chocolate
75g milk chocolate

1. Line a 450g loaf tin with greaseproof paper. Separate the eggs, keeping each white in a separate bowl.
2. Place the egg yolks and sugar in a bowl and mix well. Put the milk in a saucepan and heat gently until almost boiling. Pour the milk on to the egg yolks, whisking until combined.
3. Place the bowl over a pot of simmering water and stir until the mixture coats the back of a spoon. Drop in the gelatine and stir until combined.
4. Whip the cream until it is just holding its shape. Fold into the egg custard. Then divide the mixture into 3.
5. Melt the 3 types of chocolate separately and set aside. Add dark chocolate to one of the bowls of custard. Whip one of the egg whites and combine. Place in the loaf tin and put in a fridge for 15 minutes or until slightly set.
6. Repeat with white chocolate and then the milk chocolate.
7. Allow to set in a fridge for at least 2 hours.
8. Remove from the fridge and slice with a hot knife and serve.

Fresh berry roulade

Serves 6 - 8

4 egg whites
250g caster sugar
375ml whipped cream
125g strawberries
125g raspberries
30g melted dark chocolate, to decorate

1. Pre-heat the oven to 150°C/300°F/Gas 2.
2. Line a baking tray with greaseproof paper.
3. Place the egg whites in a large bowl (dry stainless steel), leave to come to room temperature and then whip until they form soft peaks. Gradually add in the sugar. Don't over-mix or the mixture will become grainy.
4. Spread the mixture evenly on the paper. Bake for 10 to 15 minutes and allow to cool.
5. To roll the roulade the key is confidence - you need to be firm but gentle. Sieve some icing sugar onto another sheet of greaseproof paper in an even layer, then turn the meringue out on top of the icing sugar. Remove old paper.
6. Spread the cream evenly over the top and add berries (reserve a few for decoration). Roll up, using the sheet of greaseproof paper to help you lift the meringue and transfer to a serving plate. Decorate with the reserved strawberries and raspberries.

Chocolate and chestnut marquise

Serves 4

7 egg yolks
165g caster sugar
200g 70% cocoa solid dark chocolate, roughly chopped
250g butter, softened
65g cocoa powder, sifted
400ml cream
200ml chestnut purée
1 tsp vanilla essence

1. Line a 1 litre capacity terrine mould with cling film, leaving the excess to hang over the sides. Or if you prefer, use individual moulds.
2. Beat the egg yolks and sugar in a heatproof bowl with a mixer for 5 minutes or until thick and light in colour. Place the bowl over a pan of simmering water (make sure the bowl doesn't touch the water).
3. Add the chocolate and whisk until melted. Add the butter a little at a time, whisking until smooth.
4. Remove from heat and fold in the cocoa.
5. Beat the cream and vanilla essence until soft peaks form, then mix with the chestnut purée.
6. Fold a little cream into the chocolate mixture. Fold in remainder until combined.
7. Pour into the mould, fold over plastic wrap to cover, then place in a fridge overnight.
8. Turn out to serve and dust with cocoa powder.

143

Truffle cake

Serves 8 - 10

170ml whipping cream
600g 70% cocoa solid chocolate, chopped*
8 – 10 tbsp unsweetened cocoa

1. Bring the cream to the boil and remove from heat.
2. Add the chopped chocolate and dissolve. Place mixture in a lined cake tin and allow to set.
3. To remove, run a hot knife around the edge and place on a plate. Dust with cocoa powder.

* The quality of chocolate you use will have a big effect on the end product. So, if you like it dark, use the 70% cocoa solid chocolate or, if that's too bitter, simply reduce the cocoa content of the chocolate to suit your taste.

Pistachio truffles

170ml whipping cream
600g 46% cocoa solid chocolate
50g pistachio nuts, shelled and chopped
8 – 10 tbsp unsweetened cocoa

1. Bring the cream to the boil and remove from heat.
2. Add chopped chocolate and dissolve.
3. Add pistachio nuts and chill.
4. Use a spoon to portion truffles, then roll in cocoa to shape into balls.

147

"A great accompaniment to coffee or drinks."

Ever-popular recipes –
& easy to make too!

Cooking
with Kids

Pizza

Makes 16 kids' pizzas or 8 adult pizzas

Pizza base

1kg strong bakers' flour
1 tbsp salt
2 x 7g sachets of dried yeast
600ml lukewarm water
1 tbsp sugar
4 tbsp olive oil

1. Pre-heat the oven to 220°C/425°F/Gas 7.
2. Dissolve the yeast in the lukewarm water and add the sugar.
3. Combine the flour and salt and put into a large bowl.
4. Add the yeast mixture and olive oil and combine well.
5. Knead for 10 minutes and rest for 15 minutes.
6. Divide into 16 pieces and roll to 2cm thick.
7. Add tomato sauce, then toppings.
8. Cook for 8-10 minutes

Tomato sauce

1kg ripe tomatoes, chopped
1 medium onion, diced
3 cloves of garlic, crushed
2 tbsp olive oil

1. Cook the onion in a medium pot with olive oil until soft and add the chopped tomatoes. Cook slowly for about 25 minutes or until it has thickened.
2. Add the garlic and cook for 5 minutes more.
3. Blend and pass through a sieve to remove seeds and skin.

As far as I am concerned anything goes with pizza so don't be afraid to experiment. You can go with the classics such as ham and pineapple or chicken and sweetcorn. But I have to say one of my favourites is buffalo mozzarella and basil leaves with a little sun blushed tomato and a little pesto. If you can get your kids eating this it's great. Pizzas are a wonderful way of getting children to eat certain foods that on their own they wouldn't dream of trying.

FLOUR

151

Gingerbread men

250g unsalted butter
90g brown sugar
2 tbsp ground ginger
2 tsp ground cinnamon
3 tsp finely grated lemon zest
525g golden syrup
230g honey
3 eggs, beaten
1kg plain flour
2 tsp bicarbonate of soda
½ tsp salt

1. Pre-heat the oven to 170°C/325°F/Gas 3.
2. Cream the butter and sugar, add the lemon zest and spices.
3. Boil the golden syrup and honey, cool for 10 minutes then add to the creamed mixture.
4. Add the eggs and beat well.
5. Sift the dry ingredients together and add to the mixture. Chill for 30 minutes.
6. Roll out to 2cm thickness and use a gingerbread cutter to cut out. Place on a floured non-stick tray and cook for about 12 minutes or until golden. Cool and decorate.

To decorate:

200g icing sugar
a few tsps of water
food colouring, various colours

1. Mix the sugar with the water a little at a time into a thick paste.
2. Divide the icing into three in bowls and add a few drops of different food colouring to each.
3. Pipe the icing to create faces and bow ties for boys and skirts for girls. A drop of icing will also glue jellies or smarties on as buttons.

"Great to get the kids cooking.
The trick is to involve the kids
and have fun."

Strawberry shortbread with pastry cream

Serves 4

Pastry cream

500ml milk
½ vanilla bean, split lengthwise, remove seeds and reserve
3 large egg yolks
100g granulated white sugar
25g plain flour
25g cornflour

1. Bring the milk to the boil and put to one side. Combine the egg yolks and the sugar.
2. Sift and combine the flour and cornflour, then mix into the eggs.
3. Add the milk and vanilla seeds, then stir. Return to the heat and cook for 5 minutes, continually stirring. Strain into a bowl, cover and refrigerate.

Shortbread

100g plain flour
pinch of salt
100g unsalted butter, cubed and left to soften
50g caster sugar
1 egg yolk
1 tsp vanilla essence
1 egg, beaten
16 strawberries

1. Preheat oven to 180°C/350°F/Gas 4.
2. Sift the flour and salt.
3. Make a well and add the butter, sugar, egg yolk, cream and vanilla essence. Combine and gently incorporate flour. Wrap in cling-film and refrigerate for 2 hours.
4. Roll out and cut biscuits. Eggwash and bake on a sheet of greaseproof paper until pale golden for 15 to 18 minutes.
5. To finish, lay out half the shortbread on a tray. Pipe on pastry cream. Decorate with strawberries and place shortbread on top.

Strawberry smoothie

Serves 3 - 4

You can make many different types of smoothies. Don't feel restricted. Experiment and have fun. There is no set deal or rule to follow. Below is a guideline of what I do myself at home with my nieces (well, for myself, but it's good to have an excuse!).

> *12 strawberries*
> *1 banana*
> *½ pineapple*
> *2 scoops vanilla ice cream*
> *1 cup orange juice*
> *1 tbsp maple syrup*

1. All you do is skin and roughly chop all of the fruit and place it into the blender.
2. Then pour in the orange juice, add the 2 scoops of ice cream and the tablespoon of maple syrup, cover and blitz.
3. Remove and pour into a glass. Sit back and relax.

Selection box smoothie

Go with the recipe above but take out the pineapple and add a bar from a selection box instead. But don't go with Turkish delight - it doesn't work, trust me.

This is great fun with the kids and a good way to get them to eat fruit. A healthier option would be to replace the ice cream with 4 or 5 ice cubes and a scoop of Greek yogurt.

157

Cupcakes

Makes 12 cupcakes

200g plain flour
160g butter
160g brown sugar
150ml cream
3 eggs
1 tsp baking powder
1 tsp vanilla essence
12 paper cupcake cases

1. Pre-heat oven to 180°C/350°F/Gas 4.
2. Line a muffin tin with the paper cases.
3. Cream the butter and sugar together until light and fluffy and add the vanilla essence.
4. Add the eggs one by one and beat well.
5. Sift the flour and baking powder into a separate bowl, then fold into the egg mixture to prevent curdling.
6. Spoon the mixture into the paper cases and bake for 20 – 25 minutes.

Frosting

150g cream cheese
150g mascarpone cheese
2 tsp vanilla essence
zest of ½ a lemon
200g icing sugar

1. Mix the cream cheese and mascarpone. Then sift in the icing sugar. Add the lemon zest and vanilla essence and beat for 5 minutes.
2. If making chocolate frosting, replace 20g of the sugar with 20g of cocoa or use a few drops of food colouring to alter the colour.

If you wish you can add fresh fruit or small pieces of chocolate or chocolate chips after stage 3 of the recipe for the cupcakes.

Sophistication in a glass!

Cocktails

Mulled wine

1 bottle dry red wine - burgundy is probably
best but there is no need to use hugely expensive
wines
1 lemon, halved
200ml orange juice
½ cup sugar
2 cinnamon sticks
4-5 whole cloves
½ tbsp nutmeg, grated
50ml brandy

1. In a large-bottomed pot, combine 1 lemon (halved and studded with the cloves), sugar, cinnamon sticks, orange juice, brandy and the bottle of red wine.
2. Bring to the boil and reduce heat to a gentle simmer for about 30 to 45 minutes.
3. Grate in a little nutmeg and serve warm in a wine glass. Now sit back and relax!

Eggnog

6 eggs, separated
3 cups milk
2 cups cream – full fat
2 cups whiskey – a bourbon like Jim Beam is best
⅔ cups sugar
⅓ cup brandy
2 tsp ground nutmeg

1. In a large bowl and using a mixer, beat the egg yolks together with the sugar for approximately 10 minutes (the mixture should be firm and the colour of butter).
2. Very slowly, add in the whiskey and brandy – just a little at a time. When the whiskey and brandy have been added, allow the mixture to cool in the fridge (for up to 6 hours, depending on how long before your party you're making the eggnog). Then, 30 minutes before your guests arrive, stir the milk into the chilled yolk mixture and then stir in the ground nutmeg.
3. In a separate bowl, beat the cream with a mixer on high speed until the cream forms stiff peaks.
4. In yet another bowl, beat the egg whites until stiff peaks form.
5. Gently fold the egg whites into the egg yolk mixture, then gently fold the cream into the egg mixture.
6. After ladling into cups, garnish with a little extra ground nutmeg.

Warm cinnamon cider

Serves 4

1 litre cider
100ml Jameson whiskey
6 - 7 cinnamon sticks
1 orange, quartered
2 apples, quartered
½ tsp of ground ginger
½ tsp of ground nutmeg
8 - 9 whole cloves

1. Stud the quartered apples with the whole cloves and add to a saucepan along with the cider, orange, 2 cinnamon sticks, ginger and nutmeg.
2. Bring to the boil and reduce heat to a simmer. Add the whiskey. Pour into a tall handled glass, using the remaining cinnamon sticks as a garnish.

Easy and tasty.

Bloody Mary

1 shot of vodka - from the freezer, always better
380ml tomato juice
juice of 1 lemon
2 drops Worcestershire sauce
2 drops of Tabasco
Celery stick for garnish

1. Add all the ingredients to a cocktail shaker with ice and shake well.
2. Strain the mixture into a tall ice-filled glass. Sit back!

Raspberry and chocolate flavoured espresso martini

40ml raspberry vodka*
1 shot espresso
25ml Tia Maria
1 lemon wedge
2 tbsp of icing sugar
a handful of good quality chocolate, finely grated

1. Rub the outside rim of a martini glass with the lemon wedge. In a saucer, mix the icing sugar with a sprinkle of grated chocolate. Now dip the martini glass into the saucer to coat the outside rim.
2. In an ice-filled shaker, add the vodka, espresso and Tia Maria. Shake and strain into the martini glass. The mixture should be frothy on top, to which can be added another sprinkle of grated chocolate.

* Raspberry vodka – To make, simply add two handfuls of fresh raspberries to a bottle of vodka. The vodka will preserve the raspberries and, in turn, the raspberries will flavour the vodka. Try making your own flavours. A sliced vanilla pod or a few chillies for a little kick work very well.

"This is the simple classic recipe for a Bloody Mary."

Brandy Alexander

30ml brandy
20ml Crème de Cacao – dark not white
30ml pouring cream
nutmeg

1. Pour all ingredients into an ice-filled shaker and shake vigorously. Strain into a chilled martini glass and grate over a little nutmeg.
2. If you do not have Crème de Cacao, try substituting with a coffee-based liqueur like Tia Maria or Kahlua.

Cranberry mojito

10 mint leaves
2 sugar cubes
½ lime, cut into wedges
40ml white rum
100ml cranberry juice
dash of sugar syrup*
small handful of cranberries
sprig of mint to garnish

1. In a tall glass, muddle** together the mint, lime, cranberries, sugar cubes and sugar syrup.
2. Fill half the glass with crushed ice and stir.
3. Add the rum and fill the glass to the brim with crushed ice.
4. Pour over the cranberry juice and garnish with a mint sprig.

* Sugar syrup – half-fill a clean wine bottle with sugar (brown is best) and fill the bottle with boiling water. Seal and shake vigorously until the sugar is dissolved. This is also known as 'simple syrup' or 'gomme syrup' and is used in many cocktail recipes.

** Muddle – similar to how you would use a pestle and mortar. Use the handle of a wooden spoon to push down and twist to mix the ingredients.

Champagne cocktails
Mimosa

1 bottle good champagne, chilled
750ml orange juice
cranberry juice - optional

1. Fill a champagne glass a third-full of orange juice, then fill with the champagne. So easy, sooooo tasty!

For a great addition to this, add a dash of cranberry juice into the basic mimosa.

Bellini

1 bottle good champagne, chilled
peach purée - to taste
raspberry purée - to taste

1. Fill a champagne glass three quarters full and add a small amount of both the peach and raspberry purée. It is best to make the Bellini to taste, so add as little or much purée as you wish!

If you don't have any purée, just use any peach schnapps instead. Again, add to the champagne according to your tastebuds.

Quick & easy – and delicious, too!

Brunches

Eggs Benedict (my way!)

Serves 4

Hollandaise sauce:
150g butter, melted
1 egg yolk
1 tbsp white wine vinegar

8 slices of smoked streaky bacon
8 eggs
8 slices of brioche or 4 English muffins, halved
salt & black pepper

1. For the hollandaise sauce, place a large bowl over a pot of simmering water.
2. Add the vinegar and egg yolks and whisk until the mixture thickens (until it coats the back of a spoon).
3. Gradually add in the melted butter, very slowly at the beginning, whisking continuously until all is incorporated (if the mixture gets too thick, add a little water to correct the consistency).
4. Place the bacon under the grill until crispy.
5. Then poach the eggs in simmering water with a dash of vinegar. While the eggs are poaching, toast the brioche.
6. To plate the dish, place the brioche on a plate, top it with the bacon then the poached eggs. Drizzle with the hollandaise sauce. Season with salt and black pepper and serve.

"I love this on a lazy day at home."

Breakfast mushrooms

Serves 4

Hollandaise sauce:
150g butter, melted
1 egg yolk
1tbsp white wine vinegar

8 portobello mushrooms
2 peppers, diced
1 small bunch of parsley, chopped
good quality olive oil
sea salt & black pepper

1. Preheat the oven to 180°C/350°F/Gas 4.
2. For the hollandaise sauce, place a large bowl over a pot of simmering water, add the vinegar and egg yolks and whisk until the mixture thickens (until it coats the back of a spoon).
3. Gradually add in the melted butter, very slowly at the beginning, whisking continuously until all is incorporated (if the mixture gets too thick, add a little water to correct the consistency).
4. Place the mushrooms and diced peppers on a tray and drizzle with a little olive oil and salt and pepper. Place in the oven for 8 minutes and remove. Place mushrooms on a plate, then cover generously with hollandaise sauce, then the peppers and parsley and serve.

"*Similar to Eggs Benedict I know, but a nice variation for vegetarians.*"

BLT

Serves 4

8 slices of bacon
2 tomatoes, sliced
2 tbsp mayonnaise
¼ head iceberg lettuce
4 soft flour baps
2 chicken breasts, cooked and sliced

1. Place bacon under the grill until crispy, then toast the baps.
2. Spread mayonnaise onto the bread. Then add the chicken, lettuce, tomato and bacon, finish with the top of the buns spread with mayonnaise.

177

Pancakes

Serves 4

150g plain flour
1 tsp baking powder
½ tsp salt
2 tbsp caster sugar
150ml milk
1 egg, beaten
2 tbsp butter, melted

1. Sift the flour, baking powder, salt and caster sugar into a large bowl.
2. Mix the milk and egg, then whisk in the melted butter.
3. Add the milk mix into the flour mixture and beat until you have a smooth batter.
4. Heat a frying pan over a medium heat and add a knob of butter. When it's melted, add a ladle of batter and cook until the top of the pancake begins to bubble, then turn it over and cook until both sides are golden-brown. Repeat until all the batter is used.

Steak sandwich

Serves 4

*4 sirloin steaks - approximately 180g - 200g
each (I find sirloin works best as there is very
little fat)
8 slices crusty white bread
12 cherry tomatoes, quartered
2 handfuls of rocket
1 onion, sliced
8 button mushrooms, sliced
olive oil
sea salt & cracked pepper
balsamic vinegar
garlic butter – see page 196*

1. Sauté the sliced onions and mushrooms in a hot pan, using a little of the garlic butter. When cooked, remove to the side.
2. Place the pan back on the heat, coat the steaks with some olive oil, sea salt and cracked black pepper and place into the pan, cooking on each side for about 3 minutes each.
3. While the steaks are cooking, very lightly toast the bread, mix the rocket with the quartered cherry tomatoes, some sea salt, cracked pepper, a drizzle of olive oil and a little balsamic vinegar.
4. Construct the dish as follows: Slice the steak into 4 pieces and lay on a slice of bread. Top the steak with mushroom and onions and then with a little of the rocket salad. Top with the other slice of bread. Serve with garlic butter or if you prefer, for earlier in the day, just give the toast a brush with some real butter.

"Any excuse will do to have a steak sandwich but I do think it is a great morning-after dish as it hits all the right notes for what you want when you're suffering just a little."

*Little snacks – to stave off hunger
pangs and fill any lingering gaps!*

Buffet Bites

Baby goats' cheese tarts

Makes 12 tartlets

12 large cherry tomatoes – 1 per tartlet
1 tsp caster sugar
1 crushed clove garlic
12 fresh oregano leaves, chopped
olive oil
cracked pepper
sea salt
325g puff pastry
150g goats' cheese – personally, I use Ardsallagh

1. Pre-heat the oven to 200°C/450°F/Gas 6.
2. Then cut the tomatoes into halves and lay out on tin-foil on a baking tray.
3. Next, mix the sugar, garlic, oregano, salt and pepper and sprinkle over the cherry tomatoes.
4. Then drizzle with the olive oil and place into the oven and leave for about 25 minutes until the tomatoes are soft and juicy. Remove from the oven and leave to cool.
5. Roll out the puff pastry until it's about 3 or 4mm thick. Next, take an edged cookie-cutter (around 7 cm is a good size) and cut out 12 discs. Then prick each disc with a fork and place 2 pieces of cherry tomato, cut side up, on each one.
6. Place on to the baking tray and put back in the oven for around 8 minutes or until they are just cooked.
7. While they are cooking, dice the cheese into around 1cm pieces. Place the cubes of cheese onto the tartlets and leave to cook for a further 2 to 3 minutes. Serve.

Air-dried beef bruschetta

1 full length baguette, nice & crusty
12 slices air-dried beef
120g horseradish cream
120g pickled red onion – see page 194

Cut the baguette into 12 thin angular slices. Spread the horseradish cream over each slice. Place a folded slice of the beef on the bread and finish with a little of the pickled red onion. Spread out onto a platter and serve.

"Again, this is a dish designed for party food. It's simple, effective and can be made up a little in advance."

Grandma Chow's crispy crab wontons

Makes 20

packet of wonton skins – buy from your local oriental store

150g cooked and picked crab meat

½ tsp fresh ginger, grated

1 clove of garlic, finely chopped

2 spring onions, very finely chopped

1 tbsp sweet soy sauce

sea salt

cracked pepper

half a handful of coriander, finely chopped

1 egg

50ml milk

2 tbsp flour

sweet chilli sauce – optional

plum sauce – optional

sunflower oil for frying

1. For the eggwash, crack the egg into a small bowl, add the milk and whisk well.
2. For the crab mix, place the crab, ginger, garlic, spring onions, coriander and soy sauce in a bowl and mix well. Add seasoning to taste.
3. Next, lay out 20 wonton skins on a flat surface, lightly dusted with flour to help prevent sticking. Very lightly, brush the edge of the wonton all the way around the square with the eggwash, using a pastry brush.
4. Then place some of the crab mix, about the size of a thumbnail, into the centre of the wonton. Catch the bottom right-hand corner of the pastry and fold over until it joins with the top left corner, creating a triangle. Push down the 3 sides, forming a seal with a bubble of crab in the centre (don't push on this).
5. Place the wonton on a sheet of greaseproof paper on a tray. Repeat the process until finished - it is worth it. Do this one at a time because otherwise the pastry will get too soggy and will not cook properly.
6. Place the wontons out flat on the tray, cover with another sheet of greaseproof paper and wrap with cling-film and place in the freezer. These will keep easily for a month.
7. To serve, all you need to do is deep-fry from frozen. Do not over-crowd the fryer. The wontons will crisp up and go golden brown in 2 minutes. Drain well. Serve in a bowl with a dipping sauce, maybe a sweet chilli or a plum sauce.

"Not my grandma but I had the pleasure of working with a Chinese chef whom we christened Aubury (don't ask), from whom I have stolen this recipe. It's a great party speciality and can be made in advance and kept in a freezer until needed."

Risotto balls

300g risotto, pre-cooked - see page 110
150g flour
3 eggs
300g fresh breadcrumbs, finely crumbed
100ml milk
aïoli – optional

1. Whisk the eggs and milk together in a bowl.
2. Now divide the risotto mix into roughly 50g balls. Roll the risotto balls in flour and eggwash.
3. Then toss the balls in the breadcrumbs to give an even, all-round coating.
4. Deep-fry the risotto balls for 4 to 5 minutes until golden brown and heated through.

You can serve with aïoli to enhance the flavour, but this is not essential.

189

New Year's Eve prawns and salsa

This is a variation on the starter dish on page 70

1. Follow the recipe until the serving suggestion.
2. What I recommend for New Year's Eve is that you purchase a dozen Chinese serving spoons, which can be found at any Chinese market.
3. In each spoon, place a serving of the salsa and, on top of this, place a prawn standing up. Then place these spoons on a rectangular serving plate. I guarantee these will make a great talking point on the night.

191

Stock items that you should always have to hand.

For Your Larder

Pickles

500ml water
300ml vinegar
150g sugar
a few peppercorns
a few juniper berries
1 bay leaf

Pickling liquor

Place all ingredients in a saucepan and bring to the boil. Remove from heat and leave to cool.

Pickled cucumber

Finely slice a cucumber, season with salt and leave overnight. Rinse off salt, place in a sealing jar, cover with pickling liquor and seal.

Pickled ginger

Peel the ginger using a teaspoon (trust me, it's the best tool). Finely slice it and place in a jar. Cover with pickling liquor and seal.

Pickled red onion

Slice 6 red onions into rings and place into jar. Cover with pickling liquor and seal.

All-purpose base stock

Basically, this is a base stock made from the trimmings of the vegetables you are using. It is perfectly fine to use fresh vegetables - it just costs more!
Suitable vegetables are onions, leeks, carrots and celery. Stay away from aubergine, courgette and turnip, as these are not compatible at all.

1. Place a pot on a high heat. Add a drizzle of olive oil and add the vegetable trimmings (or the roughly chopped vegetables), some fresh herbs and a bay leaf.
2. Turn down the heat and let the vegetables sweat for a couple of minutes.
3. Next, add the water - about 5 times the level of the vegetables and bring to the boil.
4. Turn down the heat and leave to simmer for approx 90 minutes. Then strain the stock and leave to cool.

To make mushroom stock: For a quick and easy mushroom stock, use the basic stock recipe in this book, replacing the vegetables with mushrooms but changing the cooking time to about 45 minutes.

To make chicken stock: At the sweating off stage, just add a chicken carcass from a roast chicken (or ask your butcher for some chicken bones and complete the process the same way).

To make fish stock: Ask your fishmonger for fish bones. Tell him that it is for fish stock - he should only give you bones from flat fish as other fish are too oily and are not suitable for stock. Shells from shellfish are OK, if you wish. Again repeat the process as for base stock, adding the bones at the sweating stage but, importantly, only cook for about 30 minutes as fish stock can sour.

To make beef stock: You need to get chopped up beef bones from your butcher. Ask him to get them down to a nice handy size, no more than 10cm if possible, as obviously beef bones are very large. Next, smear the bones with a little tomato purée, place on a baking tray and cook in a pre-heated oven at 200°C/400°F/Gas 6 for about 30 minutes. Then make the base stock as above, substituting about ⅓ of the water with red wine and cook for about 4 hours. Skim the top of the stock to remove as much of the fat as possible.

Stocks are a great base for sauces, so it's always good to have them at hand.

They also will freeze perfectly well, so you can save time by breaking your stocks down into smaller containers. You can add the frozen stock straight to the pot.

Compound butters

Lemon and dill butter

300g butter
a good bunch of dill
1 lemon, juiced

1. Place all ingredients in a mixer or blender and purée.
2. Place mix in greaseproof paper and make into a sausage-shaped roll and refrigerate.

Thyme and garlic butter

300g butter
1 bunch of thyme, stems removed
3 cloves of garlic, crushed

1. Place all ingredients in a mixer or blender and purée.
2. Place mix in greaseproof paper and make into a sausage-shaped roll and refrigerate.

Garlic butter

300g butter
3 cloves of garlic, crushed

1. Place the ingredients in a mixer or blender and purée.
2. Place mix in greaseproof paper and make into a sausage-shaped roll and refrigerate

Brandy butter

300g butter
300g icing sugar
6 tbsp brandy

1. Beat butter and sugar until smooth.
2. Then slowly add brandy, until fully combined.
3. Place mix in greaseproof paper and make into a sausage-shaped roll and refrigerate.

"These are great time-savers and can be kept in the fridge or the freezer."

Chestnut pesto

extra virgin olive oil
200g cooked chestnuts
200g walnuts
200g grated parmesan cheese
2 handfuls flat leaf parsley
2 handfuls fresh basil leaves
juice 1 lemon
sea salt & cracked black pepper

1. Place all of the ingredients, except the oil, in a food processor and blitz.
2. Add the extra virgin olive oil, enough to form a runny consistency. Season to taste.
3. Pour the pesto into a clean dry jam jar – this will keep for a week in the fridge.

Cranberry relish

1kg cranberries
1kg sugar
1tsp cinnamon
1litre apple juice
2 whole star anise

1. Bring all ingredients to the boil, stirring often to ensure the sugar doesn't stick. Then simmer, until it reaches 110°C.
2. Test it by placing a small plate in the fridge to chill, then place a small amount of relish on top; if it sets, it's done; if it's still a little liquid, then cook for a little longer.

"*Something a little different and a bit mad but that works really well. If you wish, use pine nuts instead of the chestnuts and walnuts.*"

Curry paste

24 long red chillies
2 stalks lemongrass
12 cloves garlic
1 small ginger root
10 red shallots
2 handfuls of coriander
4 limes – juice only
1 tbsp shrimp paste

1. Remove the stalk from the chillies and cut them down the centre, removing the seeds. Then chop the chillies - roughly will do, as you will be blitzing the mix (Note: when working with chillies, make sure you don't rub your face or eyes with your hands, as you will get an irritating burn).
2. Peel the garlic cloves, ginger and shallots and roughly chop.
3. Remove the top (about 5cm) and the very bottom of the lemongrass and roughly chop (use the back of a chopping knife to soften the lemongrass before chopping).
4. Process all of the ingredients including the coriander and shrimp paste in a food processor, until a paste forms. If the lime juice hasn't loosened it enough, add a little water.

All you have to do now is put it in a clean sealed container and store in the fridge, where it will hold for 3 weeks. Great to have it done - if you get an unexpected Christmas visit from one or many, you can whip up a quick curry using this paste and the curry recipe on page 88.

"This recipe for a red curry paste can be used as a start for a curry dish or as a marinade or even mixed with some olive oil and used as a sauce. It's great with whole sea bass, a dish we use in the bistro in the Blue Haven."

Basic bread recipe

1kg strong bakers' flour
525ml warm water
30g fresh yeast – or 3 x 7g sachets dried yeast
2 tbsp sugar
1 tbsp fine sea salt
extra flour for dusting

1. Preheat the oven to 220°C/425°F/Gas 7.
2. Pile the flour into a large bowl and make a large well in the centre. Pour half the water into the well, then add the yeast, sugar and salt and stir.
3. Gradually bring in the flour from the inside of the well to the centre until you get a sticky consistency – then add the remaining water. Continue to mix until all the flour is incorporated. Flour your hands and knead the dough for 4 or 5 minutes until you have a strong and elastic dough.
4. Flour the top of your dough, cover with cling-film, and allow it to prove* for about 30 minutes until doubled in size. The colder the environment, the slower the bread will be to rise, so a warm dry area is ideal.
5. Once the dough has doubled in size, knock the air out for 30 seconds by bashing it. You can now shape it or flavour it as you like and leave it to prove for a second time for 30 minutes to an hour until it has doubled in size once more. This is very important, as the second phase will give it the lightness it requires.
6. Very gently, place the bread dough on to a flour-dusted baking tray and into the oven. Don't bang the oven door closed, as this will cause the risen bread to collapse. Bake a basic loaf at 220°C/425°F/Gas 7 for 10 minutes and then lower the oven to 180°C/350°F/Gas 4 for a further 15 minutes or until the bread has a hollow sound when tapped underneath.
7. Once cooked, place on a rack and allow it to cool for at least 30 minutes.

*To rise.

Try this for the steak sandwich or with one of the soups.

Focaccia bread

Bread dough - see page 202
1 bunch of rosemary
4 cloves of garlic
1 tbsp sea salt
100ml olive oil
12 cherry tomatoes

1. Pre-heat the oven to 180°C/350°F/Gas 4.
2. At stage 4 of the basic bread recipe, knock back the dough as described and then roll to a thickness of about 1 to 1½ inches. Use your fingers to prod holes in the bread.
3. Take the rosemary off the stalk, crush the 4 cloves of garlic and half the cherry tomatoes. Combine with the olive oil and sea salt and gently rub the mix onto the surface of the bread (as the bread bakes, the rosemary will release its own oils and combine with the olive oil and be absorbed).
4. Allow the bread to prove - see stage 4 and 5 of the previous recipe. Then bake for 15 to 20 minutes until golden. Remove from the oven and allow to cool on a wire rack.

"A staple of every meal."

Index